Moo

by Iain Gray

Lang**Syne**

PUBLISHING

WRITING *to* REMEMBER

Lang**Syne**

PUBLISHING

WRITING *to* REMEMBER

79 Main Street, Newtongrange,
Midlothian EH22 4NA
Tel: 0131 344 0414   Fax: 0845 075 6085
E-mail: info@lang-syne.co.uk
www.langsyneshop.co.uk

Design by Dorothy Meikle
Printed by Printwell Ltd
© Lang Syne Publishers Ltd 2017

ISBN 978-1-85217-302-9

Moore

MOTTO:
Conlan forever.

CREST:
A hand holding a sword
piercing three gory heads.

NAME variations include:
Ó Mordha *(Gaelic)*
O'Moore
O'More
Morey
Moor
More
Muir

Chapter one:
Origins of Irish surnames

According to an old saying, there are two types of Irish – those who actually are Irish and those who wish they were.

This sentiment is only one example of the allure that the high romance and drama of the proud nation's history holds for thousands of people scattered across the world today.

It's a sad fact, however, that the vast majority of Irish surnames are found far beyond Irish shores, rather than on the Emerald Isle itself.

The population stood at around eight million souls in 1841, but today it stands at fewer than six million.

This is mainly a tragic consequence of the potato famine, also known as the Great Hunger, which devastated Ireland between 1845 and 1849.

The Irish peasantry had become almost wholly reliant for basic sustenance on the potato, first introduced from the Americas in the seventeenth century.

When the crop was hit by a blight, at least 800,000 people starved to death while an estimated two million others were forced to seek a new life far from their native shores – particularly in America, Canada, and Australia.

The effects of the potato blight continued until about 1851, by which time a firm pattern of emigration had become established.

Ireland's loss, however, was to the gain of the countries in which the immigrants settled, contributing enormously, as their descendants do today, to the well being of the nations in which their forefathers settled.

But those who were forced through dire circumstance to establish a new life in foreign parts never forgot their roots, or the proud heritage and traditions of the land that gave them birth.

Nor do their descendants.

It is a heritage that is inextricably bound up in the colourful variety of Irish names themselves – and the origin and history of these names forms an integral part of the vibrant drama that is the nation's history, one of both glorious fortune and tragic misfortune.

This history is well documented, and one of the most important and fascinating of the earliest sources are *The Annals of the Four Masters*, compiled between 1632 and 1636 by four friars at the Franciscan Monastery in County Donegal.

Compiled from earlier sources, and purporting to go back to the Biblical Deluge, much of the material takes in the mythological origins and history of Ireland and the Irish.

This includes tales of successive waves of invaders and settlers such as the Fomorians, the Partholonians, the Nemedians, the Fir Bolgs, the Tuatha De Danann, and the Laigain.

Of particular interest are the *Milesian Genealogies*,

because the majority of Irish clans today claim a descent from either Heremon, Ir, or Heber – three of the sons of Milesius, a king of what is now modern day Spain.

These sons invaded Ireland in the second millennium B.C, apparently in fulfilment of a mysterious prophecy received by their father.

This Milesian lineage is said to have ruled Ireland for nearly 3,000 years, until the island came under the sway of England's King Henry II in 1171 following what is known as the Cambro-Norman invasion.

This is an important date not only in Irish history in general, but for the effect the invasion subsequently had for Irish surnames.

'Cambro' comes from the Welsh, and 'Cambro-Norman' describes those Welsh knights of Norman origin who invaded Ireland.

But they were invaders who stayed, inter-marrying with the native Irish population and founding their own proud dynasties that bore Cambro-Norman names such as Archer, Barbour, Brannagh, Fitzgerald, Fitzgibbon, Fleming, Joyce, Plunkett, and Walsh – to name only a few.

These 'Cambro-Norman' surnames that still flourish throughout the world today form one of the three main categories in which Irish names can be placed – those of Gaelic-Irish, Cambro-Norman, and Anglo-Irish.

Previous to the Cambro-Norman invasion of the twelfth century, and throughout the earlier invasions and settlement of those wild bands of sea rovers known as the Vikings in the eighth and ninth centuries, the population of the island was relatively small, and it was normal for a person to be identified through the use of only a forename.

But as population gradually increased and there were many more people with the same forename, surnames were adopted to distinguish one person, or one community, from another.

Individuals identified themselves with their own particular tribe, or 'tuath', and this tribe – that also became known as a clann, or clan – took its name from some distinguished ancestor who had founded the clan.

The Gaelic-Irish form of the name Kelly, for example, is Ó Ceallaigh, or O'Kelly, indicating descent from an original 'Ceallaigh', with the 'O' denoting 'grandson of.' The name was later anglicised to Kelly.

The prefix 'Mac' or 'Mc', meanwhile, as with the clans of the Scottish Highlands, denotes 'son of.'

Although the Irish clans had much in common with their Scottish counterparts, one important difference lies in what are known as 'septs', or branches, of the clan.

Septs of Scottish clans were groups who often bore an entirely different name from the clan name but were under the clan's protection.

In Ireland, septs were groups that shared the same name and who could be found scattered throughout the four provinces of Ulster, Leinster, Munster, and Connacht.

The 'golden age' of the Gaelic-Irish clans, infused as their veins were with the blood of Celts, pre-dates the Viking invasions of the eighth and ninth centuries and the Norman invasion of the twelfth century, and the sacred heart of the country was the Hill of Tara, near the River Boyne, in County Meath.

Known in Gaelic as 'Teamhar na Rí', or Hill of Kings, it was the royal seat of the 'Ard Rí Éireann', or High King of Ireland, to whom the petty kings, or chieftains, from the island's provinces were ultimately subordinate.

It was on the Hill of Tara, beside a stone pillar known as the Irish 'Lia Fáil', or Stone of Destiny, that the High Kings were inaugurated and, according to legend, this stone would emit a piercing screech that could be heard all over Ireland when touched by the hand of the rightful king.

The Hill of Tara is today one of the island's main tourist attractions.

Opposition to English rule over Ireland, established in the wake of the Cambro-Norman invasion, broke out frequently and the harsh solution adopted by the powerful forces of the Crown was to forcibly evict the native Irish from their lands.

These lands were then granted to Protestant colonists, or 'planters', from Britain.

Many of these colonists, ironically, came from Scotland and were the descendants of the original 'Scotti', or 'Scots', who gave their name to Scotland after migrating there in the fifth century A.D., from the north of Ireland.

Colonisation entailed harsh penal laws being imposed on the majority of the native Irish population, stripping them practically of all of their rights.

The Crown's main bastion in Ireland was Dublin and its environs, known as the Pale, and it was the dispossessed peasantry who lived outside this Pale, desperately striving to eke out a meagre living.

It was this that gave rise to the modern-day expression of someone or something being 'beyond the pale'.

Attempts were made to stamp out all aspects of the ancient Gaelic-Irish culture, to the extent that even to bear a Gaelic-Irish name was to invite discrimination.

This is why many Gaelic-Irish names were anglicised with, for example, and noted above, Ó Ceallaigh, or O'Kelly, being anglicised to Kelly.

Succeeding centuries have seen strong revivals of Gaelic-Irish consciousness, however, and this has led to many families reverting back to the original form of their name, while the language itself is frequently found on the fluent tongues of an estimated 90,000 to 145,000 of the island's population.

Ireland's turbulent history of religious and political strife is one that lasted well into the twentieth century, a landmark century that saw the partition of the island into the twenty-six counties of the independent Republic of

Ireland, or Eire, and the six counties of Northern Ireland, or Ulster.

Dublin, originally founded by Vikings, is now a vibrant and truly cosmopolitan city while the proud city of Belfast is one of the jewels in the crown of Ulster.

It was Saint Patrick who first brought the light of Christianity to Ireland in the fifth century A.D.

Interpretations of this Christian message have varied over the centuries, often leading to bitter sectarian conflict – but the many intricately sculpted Celtic Crosses found all over the island are symbolic of a unity that crosses the sectarian divide.

It is an image that fuses the 'old gods' of the Celts with Christianity.

All the signs from the early years of this new millennium indicate that sectarian strife may soon become a thing of the past – with the Irish and their many kinsfolk across the world, be they Protestant or Catholic, finding common purpose in the rich tapestry of their shared heritage.

Chapter two:

Knights of the Red Branch

Three main sources can be traced for the presence of the proud name of Moore in the Emerald Isle – a name that resonates throughout the island's long and turbulent story.

There are those Moores who first came to Ireland as adventurers in the wake of the late twelfth century Cambro-Norman invasion and the subsequent consolidation of the power of the English Crown.

These Moores, known by the native Irish as 'de Mora' and who settled mainly in the ancient province of Munster, derive their name from a term meaning 'strong mountain'.

The present day Viscounts of Drogheda trace a descent from Moores who came to hold substantial estates in Mellifont, in Co. Louth.

There was an influx in later centuries of Moores from Scotland, although the more common form of their name was Muir, or More, and were considered septs of the Scottish clans Campbell and Leslie, respectively.

But both the 'English' and 'Scottish' Moores can be considered relative newcomers to the island when compared with the ancient pedigree of those Moores who were originally known in Gaelic-Irish as Ó Mordha and, later, O'Moore or O'More.

The progenitor, or 'name father' of the Ó Mordhas was a chieftain known as Mordha, with the name thought to denote 'stately' or 'noble'.

Mordha, in turn, was in direct line of descent from one of the greatest figures in the illustrious roll call of Irish warriors – none other than Conal Cearnach, better known as Conal of the Victories.

He is a character steeped in the rich and heady brew that is Celtic myth and legend.

His father was Amairgen, famed for slaying a three-headed creature that dwelt in the underworld, while his mother was Findchaem, the daughter of a druid known as Cathbad.

But it was as a first century AD chieftain of the Craobh Ruadh, or Red Branch Knights, that Conal Cearnach achieved his own fame.

Charged with the defence of the province of Ulster, the Red Branch Knights were an aristocratic military elite whose seat was at Emain Macha, an ancient hill fort whose ruins can be seen to this day about two miles west of Armagh.

Also the seat of the kings of Ulster, Emain Macha, or Fort Navan, boasted three great halls.

One was where the king and the Red Branch Knights

feasted and slept, while another contained the province's treasury and a grisly display of the heads of slain enemies.

Finally there was the hall known as the speckled house, where the warriors' weapons were stored, while the Bron-Bherg, or Warrior's Sorrow, served as their hospital.

While Conal Cearnach was chief of the Red Branch Knights, their greatest champion was his foster brother and blood cousin Cúchulainn, known to posterity as The Hound of Ulster.

It was at Emain Macha that Cúchulainn met and fell in love with the beautiful Emer, described as 'the best maiden in Ireland', because she possessed what were known as the six precious gifts.

These were the gift of beauty, the gift of voice, the gift of sweet speech, the gift of needlework, the gift of wisdom, and the gift of chastity.

Chaste she would remain, however, refusing Cúchulainn's hand in marriage, until he had proven himself a mighty warrior.

Accordingly, he set off for the Land of Shadows, better known as the Scottish Inner Hebridean island of Skye, to receive training in the martial arts under the expert tutelage of the warrior princess known as Scathach.

His intense training lasted for a year and a day, by which time he had become an adept in skills whose true nature we can now only guess at.

They included the apple feat, the thunder feat, the feats

of the javelin and the rope, the body feat, the feat of the sword-edge and the sloped-shield, the pole throw, the noble chariot fighter's crouch, the feat of the cat, the leap over the poison stake, the breath feat, the spurt of speed, the stunning shot, and the stroke of precision.

Scathach also presented Cúchulainn with the Gae Bolg, or 'belly spear', a ferocious weapon that, once it was driven inside the victim's body, released thirty deadly barbs that ripped the stomach apart, and a magical sword, known as Caladin.

Cúchulainn was transformed into a virtual killing machine under Scathach's tutelage.

When the 'battle frenzy' took hold of him, it was said that he turned around in his skin so that his feet and knees were to the rear and his calves and buttocks to the front.

To complete this ferocious transformation, it was said that 'one eye receded into his head, the other stood out huge and red on his cheek; a man's head could go into his mouth; his hair bristled like hawthorn, with a drop of blood on each single hair; and from the ridge of his crown there arose a thick column of dark blood like the mast of a great ship.'

Cúchulainn was eventually slain in battle through an act of treachery, and it was Conal Cearnach who avenged him by killing Mosgora Mac Da Thó, king of the province of Leinster.

Not content with merely slaying his enemy, Conal then

took the dead king's brain and, mixing it with lime, made the magical slingshot known as a 'brain ball.'

With St. Fintan as their patron saint, Conal's descendants became the leading sept of what were known as 'The Seven Septs of Leix', or Laois.

One of their strongholds sat atop the forbidding Rock of Dunamase, just under five miles from present day Portlaoise, while a Cistercian abbey was founded in 1183 at what is now the township of Abbeyleix by Conor O'More, or O'Moore.

The political and military landscape of Ireland became transformed following the Cambro-Norman invasion of 1169 and the subsequent influx of English settlers and adventurers.

English dominion over the island was ratified through the Treaty of Windsor of 1175, under the terms of which Irish chieftains were only allowed to rule their territory in the role of a vassal of the king.

There were the territories of the privileged and powerful Norman barons and their retainers, the territory of the disaffected Gaelic-Irish such as the O'Moores, and the Pale – comprised of Dublin and a substantial area of its environs ruled over by an English elite.

The island groaned under a weight of oppression that was directed in the main against native Irish clans, and one indication of the harsh treatment meted out to them can be found in a desperate plea sent to Pope John XII by Roderick

O'Carroll of Ely, Donald O'Neil of Ulster, and a number of other Irish chieftains in 1318.

They stated: 'As it very constantly happens, whenever an Englishman, by perfidy or craft, kills an Irishman, however noble, or however innocent, be he clergy or layman, there is no penalty or correction enforced against the person who may be guilty of such wicked murder.

'But rather the more eminent the person killed and the higher rank which he holds among his own people, so much more is the murderer honoured and rewarded by the English, and not merely by the people at large, but also by the religious and bishops of the English race.'

The province of Ulster proved particularly stubborn in its resistance to the encroachment of the power of the English Crown, and the Ó Mordhas, or O'Mores, or O'Moores, were for centuries at the forefront of this resistance.

Chapter three:

Defenders of liberty

**An organisation founded in the U.S.A. in 1836 known as
The Ancient Order of Hibernians, and that now
functions as a Catholic Irish-American fraternal body,
traces its roots back to a Rory Oge O'Moore.**

In the words of the Order it was O'Moore who
'organised and founded Hibernianism in the year 1565 in
the county of Kildare, in the province of Leinster, and gave
his followers the name of The Defenders.'

These 'Defenders' were responsible in 1599 for one
of the greatest defeats ever inflicted on an English
Royalist army in Ireland – at the evocatively named Pass
of the Plumes, about six miles from what is now
Abbeyleix.

It was in the Pass of the Plumes that a highly disciplined
band of O'Moore guerrilla fighters and their allies killed no
less than 500 troops under the command of the Earl of
Essex.

The scene of the battle takes its name from the hundreds
of plumed English helmets that lay scattered across the
blood-soaked killing ground.

In the same year as the battle of the Pass of the Plumes
Owney Macrory O'Moore added insult to English injury by
imprisoning the powerful Duke of Ormonde.

O'Moore expressed what he thought of the English presence on his territories by releasing the duke with the humiliating addition of a millstone tied around his neck.

Matters came to an explosive head in 1641 when landowners rebelled against the English Crown's policy of settling, or 'planting' loyal Protestants on Irish land.

This policy had started during the reign from 1491 to 1547 of Henry VIII, whose Reformation effectively outlawed the established Roman Catholic faith throughout his dominions.

In the insurrection that erupted in 1641, at least 2,000 Protestant settlers were massacred, while thousands more were stripped of their belongings and driven from their lands to seek refuge where they could.

England had its own distractions with the Civil War that culminated in the execution of Charles I in 1649, and from 1641 to 1649 Ireland was ruled by a rebel group known as the Irish Catholic Confederation, or the Confederation of Kilkenny.

One of the main driving forces of this confederation was Colonel Rory O'Moore.

Terrible as the atrocities against the Protestant settlers had been, subsequent accounts became greatly exaggerated, serving to fuel a burning desire on the part of Protestants for revenge against the rebels.

The English Civil War intervened to prevent immediate action, but following the execution of Charles I and the consolidation of the power of England's Oliver Cromwell, the time was ripe was revenge.

Cromwell descended on Ireland at the head of a 20,000-strong army that landed at Ringford, near Dublin, in August of 1649.

He had three main aims: to quash all forms of rebellion, to 'remove' all Catholic landowners who had taken part in the rebellion, and to convert the native Irish to the Protestant faith.

An early warning of the terrors that were in store for the native Irish came when the northeastern town of Drogheda was stormed and taken in September and between 2,000 and 4,000 of its inhabitants killed.

The defenders of Drogheda's St. Peter's Church, who had refused to surrender, were burned to death as they huddled for refuge in the steeple and the church was deliberately torched.

Cromwell soon held the benighted land in a grip of iron, allowing him to implement what amounted to a policy of ethnic cleansing.

His troopers were given free rein to hunt down and kill priests, while rebel estates were confiscated, including those of the O'Moores whose stronghold atop the Rock of Dunamase was razed to the ground.

An edict was issued stating that any native Irish found east of the River Shannon after May 1, 1654, faced either summary execution or transportation to the West Indies.

One source that speaks of Colonel Rory O'Moore's role in the abortive rebellion states how: 'Then a private gentleman, with no resources beyond his intellect and courage, this Rory, when Ireland was weakened by defeat and confiscations... conceived the vast design of rescuing the country from England.

'History contains no stricter instance of the influence of an individual mind.'

Many native Irish such as the O'Moores were forced to seek refuge on foreign shores, and among their number was Murtagh O'Moore, who settled in France and whose descendants to this day form part of the French nobility as Lords of Valmont.

Another branch of the family who settled in Spain returned to Ireland in the mid-eighteenth century and built Moore Hall, in the province of Connacht.

It was a son of this family, John Moore, who played a brief and tragic role in the history of Ireland when it again exploded in a fury of discontent during the Rising of 1798 - an ultimately abortive attempt to restore Irish freedom and independence.

The Rising was in essence sparked off by a fusion of sectarian and agrarian unrest and a desire for political reform that had been shaped by the French revolutionary slogan of 'liberty, equality, and fraternity.'

A movement had come into existence that embraced middle-class intellectuals and the oppressed peasantry, and if this loosely bound movement could be said to have a leader, it was Wolfe Tone, a Protestant from Kildare and leading light of a radical republican movement known as the United Irishmen.

Despite attempts by the British government to concede a degree of agrarian and political reform, it was a case of far too little and much too late, and by 1795 the United Irishmen, through Wolfe Tone, were receiving help from France – Britain's enemy.

A French invasion fleet was despatched to Ireland in December of 1796, but it was scattered by storms off Bantry Bay.

Two years later, in the summer of 1798, rebellion broke out on the island, centred mainly in Co. Wexford, while a small French invasion force commanded by General Humbert landed at Killala.

The rebels achieved victory over the forces of the British Crown and militia known as yeomanry at the battle of Oulart Hill, followed by another victory at the battle of Three Rocks, but the peasant army was no match for the 20,000 troops or so that descended on Wexford.

Defeat followed at the battle of Vinegar Hill on 21 June, followed by another decisive defeat at Kilcumney Hill five days later.

On landing at Killala General Humbert had declared that Connacht was henceforth a republic and appointed John Moore as its president.

He was destined to pay dearly for this – being captured after the rebellion collapsed and dying in prison in Waterford.

Another John Moore also played a role in the 1798 Rising.

This was the British Army general Sir John Moore, who was born in Glasgow in 1761 and who commanded part of the British forces in Ireland at the time of the rebellion.

The general, who was killed in 1809 at Corunna during the Spanish Peninsular campaigns, is credited with having curbed some of the worst excesses against the defeated rebels.

Chapter four:

On the world stage

Bearers of the proud name of Moore have gained fame in a diverse array of endeavours ranging from acting and art to sport, music and literature.

Born in 1927 in Stockwell, London, **Roger Moore** was the veteran British actor who first came to prominence through his role in the television series *The Saint* that ran from 1962 to 1969.

But he is best known for his role as James Bond in no less than seven Bond movies that include *Live and Let Die*, *For Your Eyes Only*, and *A View to a Kill*.

A prominent ambassador for the children's charity U.N.I.C.E.F since 1991, he was awarded a knighthood in 2003 for his work on behalf of the organisation, while he was also awarded a C.B.E. in 1999 for his services to acting; he died in 2017.

Born in 1935 in Dagenham, London, **Dudley Moore** was the award-winning British actor, comedian, and musician, who early in his career formed one half of the 'Pete and Dud' comic double act that he formed with Peter Cook.

It was not long until Hollywood beckoned, and his film roles include *10*, co-starring Bo Derek, and the 1981 *Arthur*, for which he received an Academy Award nomination for Best Actor.

The versatile entertainer died in 2002, a year after being awarded an O.B.E

Born in Chicago in 1914 **Clayton Moore** was best known for his role as the masked man *The Lone Ranger* in the American television series of that name.

The internationally popular series featuring the Lone Ranger and his faithful friend Tonto earned an Emmy nomination in 1950, while Moore, who died in 1999, has a star on the Hollywood Walk of Fame.

Born in 1962 in Roswell, New Mexico, **Demi Moore** is the actress who was actually born Demetria Gene Guyness and who took the surname Moore from her second husband, the singer and songwriter Freddy Moore.

She married the actor Ashton Kutcher in 2005, but the couple separated in 2011.

Her film roles include the 1982 *Parasite*, the 1984 *Blame it on Rio*, the 1990 *Ghosts* and the 2011 *Margin Call*.

Married for a time to the Canadian actress Gladys Smith, better known by her stage name of Mary Pickford, **Owen Moore** was the Irish-American actor born in Fordstown Crossroads, Co. Meath, in 1886.

Immigrating to America with his brothers Joe, Tom, and Matt, who also became successful actors, Moore made 279 Hollywood movies between 1908 and 1937, including the 1909 *The Lonely Villa* and the 1937 *A Star is Born*.

In contemporary times **Mary Tyler Moore** is the

award-winning American actress best known for her role in the 1960s weekly television series *The Dick Van Dyke Show* and, in the 1970s, *The Mary Tyler Moore Show*.

Born in 1936 in Brooklyn, New York, she also appeared in the 1967 movie *Thoroughly Modern Millie*, while her awards include an Academy Award nomination and seven Emmy Awards.

Born Julie Ann Smith in Fayetteville, North Carolina, in 1960, **Julianne Moore** is the American actress whose many awards include a nomination for an Academy Award for Best Actress for the 2000 *The End of the Affair*, and a nomination for Best Supporting Actress for the 2003 *The Hours*.

Still on the stage **Constance Moore**, born in 1920 in Sioux City, Iowa, and who died in 2005, was the singer and actress who appeared in the 1939 movie serial *Buck Rogers*, while **Grace Moore**, born in Tennessee in 1898, was the American operatic actress popularly known as the Tennessee Nightingale.

Behind the camera lens **Ronald Moore**, born in 1964 in Chowchilla, California, is the award-winning American screenwriter best known for his work on *Star Trek* and the *Battlestar Galactica* television series.

A critic of globalisation, large corporations, gun violence, the American health care system, and the war in Iraq, **Michael Moore**, born in 1954, is the controversial author, film director, and producer who was raised in Flint, Michigan.

Named by Time magazine in 2005 as 'one of the world's most influential people', his hard-hitting documentaries include *Bowling for Columbine* and *Fahrenheit 9/11*.

Born in Dundalk in 1970 **John Moore** is the Irish film producer, director, and writer whose works include the 2001 *Behind Enemy Lines*, while his namesake, **John Moore**, born in Montreal in 1966, is a popular Canadian film critic, voice actor, comedian, and radio and television broadcaster.

In the world of art **Henry Moore**, born in 1898 in Castleford, Yorkshire, and who died in 1986, was the celebrated English artist and sculptor who first studied art in Leeds after service with the army during the First World War.

Inspired by the sculptures of Michelangelo, he is best known for his abstract cast bronze and carved marble sculptures, many of which now grace a number of public places across the world.

The art gallery of Ontario's Henry Moore Collection now boasts the largest public collection of his work in the world.

Born in York in 1841 **Albert Moore** was the English painter famed for his depictions of female figures set against classical world backgrounds, while his brother, **Henry Moore**, born in 1931, was a noted marine and landscape artist.

Moores have also excelled in the highly competitive sports arena.

Born in Barking in 1941 **Bobby Moore** was the English

footballer who gained iconic status as the captain of the England team that won the World Cup in the 1966 final against Germany.

The talented defender, who played for teams that included West Ham United, had won a total 108 caps playing for his country before his retirement in 1973.

Winner of the BBC Sports Personality of the Year Award following the World Cup victory, he was also awarded with an O.B.E. and made an Inaugural Inductee of the English Football Hall of Fame in 2002, nine years after his death, in recognition of his impact on the game as a player.

On the athletics track **Charles Moore, Jnr**. born in 1929 in Coatsville, Pennsylvania, is the former American athlete who took gold in the 400-metres hurdles at the 1952 Olympics.

In the boxing ring **Davey Moore**, born in New York in 1959 and who died in 1988, was the American boxer who was the world light middleweight champion from 1982 to 1983.

Also in the boxing ring Archibald Wright, born in Benoit, Mississippi in 1913, was the world light heavyweight champion between 1952 and 1959, and again in 1961, who fought under the name of **Archie Moore**.

The African-American boxer who, at the time of writing, still holds the record, at 145, for the most career knockouts of any boxer, died in 1998.

Inducted into the International Boxing Hall of Fame, he also appeared in a number of 1960s films, including *The Carpetbaggers* and *The Fortune Cookie*.

In the world of music Alecia Beth Moore is better known as the American singer and songwriter **Pink**, born in 1979 in Doylestown, Pennsylvania.

Gary Moore, born in Belfast in 1952, is the Northern Irish guitarist and songwriter who, in addition to a successful solo career, has played for such diverse artistes as Thin Lizzy, Ozzy Osbourne, and Andrew Lloyd Webber.

Born in Gadson, Tennessee, in 1931, **Scotty Moore** is the legendary American guitarist who played at one time for Elvis Presley and who is a member of the Rock and Roll Hall of Fame.

Inducted into the Louisiana Blues Hall of Fame in 2000, **Deacon John Moore** is the blues, rhythm and blues, and rock and roll musician and singer who was born in New Orleans in 1941.

In the creative world of literature **Brian Moore**, born in Belfast in 1921, was the Northern Irish novelist who won the coveted James Tait Black Memorial Prize in 1975 for *The Great Victorian Collection*.

Shortlisted for the Booker Prize on three occasions his last novel, *The Magician's Wife*, was published a year before his death in 1999.

Born in 1887 in Kirkwood, Missouri, **Marianne Moore** was the Modernist American poet and writer whose 1951

Collected Poems won a Pulitzer Prize, while **Thomas Moore** was the Irish poet born in 1779 who was the literary executor of his friend and fellow poet Lord Byron

Also a talented songwriter, he wrote the lyrics for *The Minstrel Boy* and *The Last Rose of Summer*.

Best known for his book *The Green Berets*, adapted for the 1966 film of the name starring John Wayne, **Robin Moore, Jnr.** was the American writer born in Boston in 1925 who served during the Second World War as a nose gunner in the U.S. Army Air Corps, and who was awarded the Air Medal.

He died in 2008.

One of the first women to write in the science fiction genre Catherine Lucille Moore, better known to her readers as **C.L.Moore**, was born in Indianapolis, Indiana, in 1911.

Her first stories were published in the 1930s in science fiction and fantasy magazines such as *Weird Tales* and *Astounding Science Fiction*.

It was through this that she met her future husband, the author Henry Kuttner – who had written her a fan letter in the mistaken belief that 'C.L. Moore' was a man.

The couple went on to collaborate as writers under pseudonyms that included Lewis Padgett and Lawrence O'Donnell, while their 1946 novel *Vintage Season* was filmed in 1992 as *Grand Tour*, five years after Moore's death.

Key dates in Ireland's history from the first settlers to the formation of the Irish Republic:

circa 7000 B.C.	Arrival and settlement of Stone Age people.
circa 3000 B.C.	Arrival of settlers of New Stone Age period.
circa 600 B.C.	First arrival of the Celts.
200 A.D.	Establishment of Hill of Tara, Co. Meath, as seat of the High Kings.
circa 432 A.D.	Christian mission of St. Patrick.
800-920 A.D.	Invasion and subsequent settlement of Vikings.
1002 A.D.	Brian Boru recognised as High King.
1014	Brian Boru killed at battle of Clontarf.
1169-1170	Cambro-Norman invasion of the island.
1171	Henry II claims Ireland for the English Crown.
1366	Statutes of Kilkenny ban marriage between native Irish and English.
1529-1536	England's Henry VIII embarks on religious Reformation.
1536	Earl of Kildare rebels against the Crown.
1541	Henry VIII declared King of Ireland.
1558	Accession to English throne of Elizabeth I.
1565	Battle of Affane.
1569-1573	First Desmond Rebellion.
1579-1583	Second Desmond Rebellion.
1594-1603	Nine Years War.
1606	Plantation' of Scottish and English settlers.
1607	Flight of the Earls.
1632-1636	Annals of the Four Masters compiled.
1641	Rebellion over policy of plantation and other grievances.
1649	Beginning of Cromwellian conquest.
1688	Flight into exile in France of Catholic Stuart monarch James II as Protestant Prince William of Orange invited to take throne of England along with his wife, Mary.
1689	William and Mary enthroned as joint monarchs; siege of Derry.
1690	Jacobite forces of James defeated by William at battle of the Boyne (July) and Dublin taken.

1691	Athlone taken by William; Jacobite defeats follow at Aughrim, Galway, and Limerick; conflict ends with Treaty of Limerick (October) and Irish officers allowed to leave for France.
1695	Penal laws introduced to restrict rights of Catholics; banishment of Catholic clergy.
1704	Laws introduced constricting rights of Catholics in landholding and public office.
1728	Franchise removed from Catholics.
1791	Foundation of United Irishmen republican movement.
1796	French invasion force lands in Bantry Bay.
1798	Defeat of Rising in Wexford and death of United Irishmen leaders Wolfe Tone and Lord Edward Fitzgerald.
1800	Act of Union between England and Ireland.
1803	Dublin Rising under Robert Emmet.
1829	Catholics allowed to sit in Parliament.
1845-1849	The Great Hunger: thousands starve to death as potato crop fails and thousands more emigrate.
1856	Phoenix Society founded.
1858	Irish Republican Brotherhood established.
1873	Foundation of Home Rule League.
1893	Foundation of Gaelic League.
1904	Foundation of Irish Reform Association.
1913	Dublin strikes and lockout.
1916	Easter Rising in Dublin and proclamation of an Irish Republic.
1917	Irish Parliament formed after Sinn Fein election victory.
1919-1921	War between Irish Republican Army and British Army.
1922	Irish Free State founded, while six northern counties remain part of United Kingdom as Northern Ireland, or Ulster; civil war up until 1923 between rival republican groups.
1949	Foundation of Irish Republic after all remaining constitutional links with Britain are severed.